OUR C~~AL~~ IN OXFORD

Along the Towpath from Wolvercote to Jericho and the City

Mark Davies and Catherine Robinson

Towpath Press
Oxford
1999

First published 1999

Reprinted 1999

© Mark Davies and Catherine Robinson 1999

ISBN 0 9535593 00

Published by Towpath Press, Oxford

Mark Davies, 12 Hythe Bridge Arm, Oxford Canal, Oxford OX1 2TA (tel. 01865 798254)

Designed and illustrated by Ruth Bateson

Printed by Litho & Digital Impressions Limited, Oxon

Contents

Foreword

Oxford Canal is part of a network of inland waterways which originally extended for over 3,500 miles across England and Wales. Although all the canals were built within approximately 50 years of each other, every mile of the network is unique. Built of local materials by different engineers, and developed by local companies, the nation's waterways change subtly in character from place to place.

The canal in Oxford has its own special qualities. The story of its creation, the people whose livelihoods depended on it, its heyday, and its decline are all described in this booklet. But it is not a dry collection of dusty facts: the history of the canal in Oxford is brought to life through the personal stories of the obscure but richly individual characters who lived and worked on the waterway. The booklet is, for me, alive: a warm and living testament to a fascinating past.

This publication gives me particular pleasure, since it is one of the many products of a small working group that I helped to set up in 1998, to promote public awareness of the canal in Oxford. A Consultative Forum, drawn from a broad spectrum of the community, has focused clearly on the potential of the modest canal that runs under our noses into the very heart of the city. Together we are forming a vision of the future of this canal which will benefit the citizens of Oxford and its many thousands of visitors. That future will be secure if we all, together, share responsibility for the care and enhancement of the canal, uncovering and protecting what is valuable, and building on our understanding so that future generations may enjoy the waterway as much as we do today.

Simon J. V. Ainley

Waterway Manager, Oxford and Grand Union Canals
Braunston, 1999

Preface

A step or two along the Oxford Canal towpath from Hythe Bridge Street brings an instant sense of relief. The noise, the pollution, and the traffic are forgotten in an instant, as you step into a calmer, gentler world of boats and swans, anglers and birdsong. A little farther and you come to Isis Lock, which marks the junction of the Thames and the Oxford Canal in a beautiful juxtaposition of sky and water and woodland, set off by the simplicity of the lock's gracefully curving black and white bridge and angular lock beams. Today this scene is admired by thousands of visitors prepared to take a short stroll from Hythe Bridge Street or Jericho. But the quiet setting belies a troubled, even macabre past: a past which has made it a place to avoid, a place feared and maligned practically up until the present day, as this book will explain.

Sources

Drawing on archive records, published works, oral histories, and the authors' own observations, *Our Canal in Oxford* tells the story of many of the remarkable characters associated with the Oxford Canal since it reached the city in 1790, and gives the background to the notable landmarks on the three-mile stretch between Duke's Lock and the former basin beyond Hythe Bridge. Much material has come from primary sources, most notably those of the Proprietors of the Company of the Oxford Canal Navigation, held at the Public Records Office in Kew, those of the Commissioners of the Thames Navigation, held at the Berkshire Record Office in Reading, and various other books and documents held at the Oxfordshire Archives Office and the Centre for Oxfordshire Studies.

Acknowledgements

The authors would like to thank the following people for contributing their memories and insights to the book: **Jack and Rose Skinner**, whose respective families have a long tradition

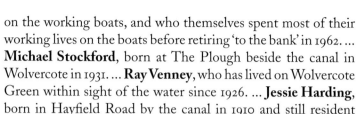

on the working boats, and who themselves spent most of their working lives on the boats before retiring 'to the bank' in 1962. ... **Michael Stockford**, born at The Plough beside the canal in Wolvercote in 1931. ... **Ray Venney**, who has lived on Wolvercote Green within sight of the water since 1926. ... **Jessie Harding**, born in Hayfield Road by the canal in 1910 and still resident there. ... **Doris Thicke**, who lived in Hayfield Road for nearly as long as Mrs Harding. ... **Sylvia Johnson**, born in a house by the canal in Kingston Road in 1908 and still there. ... **Ted Harris**, who has lived in Combe Road in Jericho for 60 years. ... **Denis Wise**, who has lived in Jericho for 44 years. ... **Ray Titcomb**, who now lives in Jericho, and his sister, **Della James**, who were both born in Upper Fisher Row and grew up there. ... Ray's wife **Jean Tustin**, the daughter of **Kath Tustin**. (Kath lived most of her life in Jericho, but moved to the Row in 1953, with her son, **Colin**, who seems certain to be the only remaining resident who can claim any blood-line back to its traditional river-barging families.) ... Kath's sister-in-law, **Pat Weller**, the daughter of Aubrey E. Tustin, who ran The Nag's Head in Hythe Bridge Street from 1932 to 1938, and again after it was rebuilt in 1939. ... **Nancy Sherratt**, one of the five daughters of the New Road wharfinger, Bernard Robinson, who raised his family in a Canal Company property on the Hythe Bridge site from 1922 to 1937, when it was sold to Nuffield College and he moved to a new position at Juxon Street Wharf in Jericho. Coincidentally, Nancy's uncle was Thomas Squires, author of a book about the parish of St Thomas which has been a major source of information for this guide.

Valuable help has also been given by British Waterways staff at Braunston and Gloucester; staff at the Centre for Oxfordshire Studies in the Westgate Library, Oxford; Professor John Barron, Master of St Peter's College; Dr K.F. Hilliard of St Peter's College; John Ashby; Barbara Huelin; and Wendy Scanlon. Ruth Bateson designed and illustrated the book, and Sophie Johnson handled the production. Thanks are due to them all, and to others, too numerous to mention, for their support and enthusiasm.

Landmarks: a note of caution

The landscape of the Oxford Canal is changing all the time. Since we began writing this book in 1998, smart new apartment blocks and town-houses have been built along the west bank of the Castle Mill Stream, and the rash of red-brick luxury developments has spread northwards along the canal, covering much of the land formerly belonging to Lucy's Ironworks on the west bank. Similar suburbanisation is soon to be the fate of Aristotle Lane. In a short time, such is the phenomenal value of land in this part of Oxford, the Unipart factory sites on both banks will be developed for 'prestige' housing. In a few years' time, Lucy's factory itself may disappear — and thus the canal's last links with its industrial past will have been broken. Despite all these changes, we hope that with the aid of the maps in this book, and the fixed landmarks of bridges and locks, readers taking real or imaginary journeys along the canal will not lose their bearings.

The authors

Mark Davies has lived on a narrowboat in central Oxford since 1992, and contributes occasional articles on life afloat to a national waterways magazine. **Catherine Robinson** has lived in Hayfield Road, within sight of the canal, since 1982. She is the author (with Elspeth Buxton) of *Hayfield Road: Nine Hundred Years of an Oxford Neighbourhood.*

We have made every effort to ensure that the contents of this guide are accurate, but would be pleased to hear from any reader with additional or conflicting information. We are keen to continue unravelling the fascinating, but largely ignored, history of our canal in Oxford.

Mark Davies and Catherine Robinson
Oxford, 1999

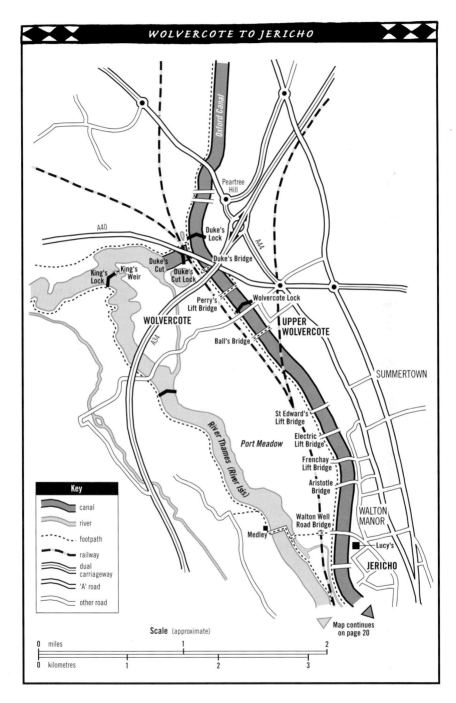

Key

	canal
	river
----	footpath
— —	railway
	dual carriageway
	'A' road
	other road

Scale (approximate)

| 0 miles | 1 | 2 |
| 0 kilometres | 1 | 2 | 3 |

Map continues on page 20

It is hard to imagine nowadays, when the Oxford Canal is a quiet backwater of villages and suburbs such as Wolvercote and Jericho, that 200 years ago it was a thriving trade route — one of the most important canals in southern England. Designed by James Brindley, the pioneering canal engineer, and his assistant Samuel Simcock, it was built by the Oxford Canal Navigation Company to provide a link with the Midlands coal fields.

Lock-keeper's cottage, a few yards south of Duke's Lock, c. 1960 with Bridge 232 spanning the eastern end of Duke's Cut in the background.

A. Watts Collection, copyright British Waterways

At the end of the 18th century, large areas of woodland had been cleared in the upper Thames valley and there was a growing demand for coal. Until 1790, coal for Oxford had to be shipped at great expense down the east coast of England from Newcastle upon Tyne, through the Port of London, and up the Thames. The impact of cheap Midlands coal on the local economy, it may be imagined, was considerable. So, presumably, was the impact on the local community of the 'navigators' or 'navvies' who dug the canal — five feet deep, 16 feet wide, all the way from Coventry — but who they were, and where they came from, we shall probably never know.

The canal reached Wolvercote in 1788, and a wharf was built on the Green. Coal from Hawkesbury Colliery near Coventry was unloaded here daily. From 1790, when the canal reached Oxford, market boats passed through Wolvercote twice a week, plying to and from Banbury; Pickford's fly boats (an express service, with frequent changes of horse) took passengers and parcels between Oxford and Banbury four times a week. Twice a week fly boats left Oxford on the six-day journey to Birmingham, and you could even travel by passenger boat to the Potteries and Merseyside. With all this traffic and trade, Wolvercote Green was a much busier place then than it is now.

Duke's Cut

In 1789, a quarter of a mile to the north of the Green, a private cut was constructed for George, the fourth Duke of Marlborough — a local landowner and a major shareholder in the Oxford Canal Company. The cut extended westwards for 500 yards, linking the canal with Wolvercote Mill Stream, a backwater of the river Thames. It gave control of traffic between the canal and the river to the Duke, who was always in need of money for the upkeep of Blenheim Palace at Woodstock. It also meant that raw materials could be delivered by boat to his paper mill, which supplied the expanding Clarendon Press in Oxford city.

Wolvercote Mill began using coal for its new steam engines in 1811. In 1856 the University (by now the owner of the mill) bought two horse-drawn narrowboats to ply to and from Moira Colliery in Leicestershire — a round trip of 218 miles — bringing 100 tons of coal each week. The mill continued to receive coal by boat till 1952, when it switched to oil. Because there was no towpath along the river to the mill, the boats had to drift backwards downstream — a dangerous operation, so close to the weir — and after unloading they were shafted back empty to the junction. Meanwhile the horse would have been taken back — probably by the boatman's eldest child — to be fed and rested in the stables at Duke's Lock (illustrated on page 1) or at the White Hart Inn in Wolvercote village.

Bridge 232, an elegant red-brick construction, still spans Duke's Cut. A flash-lock at the river end of the Cut, called

King's Lock, was designed to cope with the fluctuating level of the Thames, which could rise and fall by as much as two feet. This lock remained in use until the 1920s. Where the Cut joins the canal, there is a pound-lock, known as Duke's Cut Lock. It used to have two pairs of gates, to cope with the varying levels between canal and river; now the river is maintained at a constant level, and the lock has only one pair of gates. Until recently a wooden post stood at the entrance to the Cut, deeply grooved by the tow-lines of countless narrowboats.

A boatman photographed with his children and horse beside the Oxford Canal, c. 1900. Wooden bobbins, often painted bright colours, prevented the traces from chafing the animal's flanks.

Copyright: Oxfordshire County Council Photographic Archive

There was a well at Duke's Lock, where the boats used to take on clean drinking water. But — interviewed at length for this book — two veterans of the Oxford Canal, Rose and Jack Skinner, who were both born into the canal trade and worked a pair of boats called *Kent* and *Forget-Me-Not* in the early years of their marriage in the late 1940s, recalled that for washing most boatpeople boiled water from the canal in brass kettles on their cabin ranges.

From Duke's Lock to Wolvercote Lock

South of Duke's Lock there are **two wooden lift bridges** (or 'drawbridges'), built in the typical Oxfordshire style. The economic impact of the American War of Independence meant that the Canal Company had to save money during the construction of the canal from Banbury to Oxford; 38 minor bridges were built of timber, instead of brick or stone, which were reserved for bridges carrying wagons. Numbered 233 and 234 (counting from Longford, near Coventry), the two lift bridges south of Duke's Lock both connect with a track to the east, variously known as Nicholls' Lane, Joe White's Lane, and the Black Path, which leads to Goose Green. (Joe White, a carrier in the early years of the 20th century, lived in a now demolished house north of Goose Green.) On the east bank, opposite some now-ruined cottages on the towpath, was Drewett's Landing, where bricks from Kingerlee's brickworks in Five Mile Drive, opened in 1869, were loaded into narrowboats. In the 1930s and 1940s, in a wooden bungalow in the field behind the old landing stage, lived the Black Hat Gang. Believed to be tinkers "from London way", these eight men dabbled in scrap and always wore black trilby hats, indoors and out.

Just to the south, a brightly painted narrowboat tiller has been erected beside the towpath: a poignant memorial to Sarah Lowe and Finn and Louise — a mother and her children who died on this stretch of the canal in a fire on their narrowboat in 1996.

Bridge 235 at Wolvercote Lock is not the original bridge: that was demolished to make way for the present one, which was built to span both the canal and the Great Western Railway. (The GWR was constructed in the late 1840s, despite opposition from the Canal Company, which correctly surmised that its profits would suffer.) The area around the lock was a favourite playground of village children in the 1930s, according to Michael Stockford, who was born in 1931 at The Plough Inn on Wolvercote Green, where his father Jack was the landlord from 1929 to 1958 (and his grandfather, Herbert, before that). In a channel on the east bank (known in the dialect of Oxfordshire as 'the lasher'), which takes run-off water to the pound below the lock, the children would paddle and catch fish by hand; that was when they weren't playing in an old Bullnose Morris abandoned in a field nearby, or talking to Percy Gardiner, who lived in a romany caravan near the Black Path, earning his living by

repairing cricket bats for St Edward's School and the Oxford colleges. Smelling perpetually of the paraffin on which he ran his ancient AJS motorbike, Percy was one of the eccentric characters who led marginal lives along the banks of the canal in the days before the second world war. There seems to be less space for individualists in our present-day society — on the bank at least.

Wolvercote Green

The village children also used to play around **College Pool**, on the east bank, opposite the village hall. Known as 'the feeder', this pond collects surface water from the hillside and feeds it into the canal. It eventually filled with rushes and became derelict, but was restored in 1990 by a group of volunteers and is now a Site of Special Scientific Interest.

Just to the south of the feeder was 'the boat-turn', a V-shaped winding-hole cut into the eastern bank. According to Ray Venney, still resident on Wolvercote Green, where he was born in 1926, boats which had unloaded at Wolvercote Wharf, 200 yards farther down the canal, would be towed backwards up the canal, until level with the turn. A boatman would then shaft his boat into the turn stern-first, until it lay across the canal. His horse would then tow the boat out, allowing the boatman to steer the prow northwards, to start the return journey. It was opposite the boat-turn, one memorable day in the 1930s, that an eight-year-old boy named Dave Walker caught a pike bigger than himself.

Michael Stockford described how narrowboats would tie up on the bank near the boat-turn, waiting their turn to go down to the coal wharves of Oxford, three miles south. The women would light a fire on the bank, boil up water in a tin bath, bring out dolly tubs and mangles, and do the family wash. The men would relax with jugs of ale fetched from The Plough (they never drank in the pub, for some reason). Meanwhile the children from the boats and the boys and girls from the village would play together, paddling and catching tiddlers, collecting bulrushes (which they called 'pokers'), and messing about in a hollow elm tree called The Crocodile, to the south of The Plough. Sometimes the local children would be invited on

board the boats, which Michael Stockford recalled as spotlessly clean, with shining brasses and neat crochet work, and tiers of bunks in the cabin, to sleep as many as eight people. He remembered the canal families as "very polite".

It would be interesting to know whether the boatchildren ever attended Wolvercote School on days when their parents were laid up on the canal. Officially, the children were required to attend school and were not permitted to work on the boats before the age of 14. Unofficially, they were expected to help their parents from an early age. In the words of Rose Skinner:

> *"I was about eight when I started doing jobs for my Dad* [Alfred Hone Jnr, master of the *White City* and *Rose and Betty*]. *I used to steer the boat, standing on a stool, while my sister Bet would walk with the mule and open the lock gates. ... It was a waste of time to go to school just for an hour or two. I used to go sometimes in Longford; three of us in one desk! The teacher would give us a book and say, 'Read what you can'. Well, if you can't read, how can you read what you can? And then our Mam would come and say, 'We're loaded now, you'll have to come away'. That's all the schooling we had."*

The children must have counted themselves lucky if their parents were moored in Wolvercote at the end of August, in the week before St Giles's Fair, when Hebborn's Fair came to the Green outside The Plough, with coconut-shies and hoop-la stalls and the 'galloping horses' carousel owned by Hatwells of Cassington. At quiet times, the man in charge would give the children free rides.

On Sundays, when many locks were closed, some of the boatpeople might have attended a service in St Peter's Church, or the Baptist Church in the village. According to Jack Skinner, *"The boatpeople were religious in their own way, but we couldn't read, so we felt daft in church. My mother always went on Sundays, though, if there was one close by. And she would never throw soap-suds away on a Good Friday."* (Jack's mother was Ada Skinner, born into the Monk family, veterans of the canalboat trade, who trace their ancestry back to Thomas Monk of Dudley, one of the first canal carriers and boat builders in the 18th century, after whom the traditional narrowboats were named "monkey boats".)

Ball's Bridge and The Plough Inn

The Plough Inn dates from 1812 and probably earlier. John Ball was the landlord then. He died in 1840, aged 74, and bequeathed the pub to his daughters, who sold it. It was rebuilt in 1840, and bought by Morrell's Brewery in 1857. The stables at The Plough were used as a temporary mortuary in cases of drowning during the 19th century.

Opposite The Plough is **Wolvercote Wharf**, its stone slabs still in place, but overgrown with grass and weeds. Ray Venney watched roadstone being unloaded there from a Warwickshire quarry in his childhood; but by 1930 the wharf was used only by Henry Osborne-King, the corn merchant who lived at Church Farm. His wagons would bring hay and straw from Pixey Meadow, to be loaded on to boats and taken to the Midlands. Eventually, however, even these loads were being transported by rail: a sign of the economic decline of the canal system, which had begun with the advent of competition from the railways, and accelerated during the first world war, when many boatmen were conscripted into military service.

Immediately south of the wharf stands a brick bridge, number 236, known as **Ball's Bridge**, which leads to the railway crossing. It was over this bridge that the young Michael Stockford would go on his train-spotting expeditions. When a train was waiting on this stretch of line, he would sometimes be sent to fetch threepence-worth of ale from The Plough for the engine driver and stoker, who meanwhile would fry up eggs and bacon on their shovel in the cab.

St Edward's School Bridge

The next bridges south of Wolvercote are 237 (a brick bridge, carrying the railway line to Bicester), and then 238, a wooden drawbridge built in 1831. No track leads to it or away from it, so presumably it was constructed for the benefit of livestock passing over the canal to graze. Although it is known as **St Edward's School Bridge**, it cannot have been built for the convenience of the boys, because the school was not established on its canal-side site until 1873. One of its early pupils was Kenneth Grahame (1859–1932), who in later life earned immortality as the author of

The Wind in the Willows. It must have been along this stretch of the Oxford Canal that he first observed horse-drawn narrowboats, one of which found its way eventually into his book:

> Round a bend in the canal came plodding a solitary horse, stooping forward as if in anxious thought. From rope traces attached to his collar stretched a long line, taut, but dipping with his stride, the further part of it dripping pearly drops.

Like many people before and after him, Grahame made the mistake of calling canal boats 'barges'. Barges are wide and flat, and they work on rivers and wide canals. The boats which plied (and still ply) the lesser canals like the Oxford are called narrowboats. He was wrong, too, in calling the whiskery hero of his book 'Ratty'. Ratty, with his blunt snout, round face, and small neat ears, is not a rat but a water vole, *Arvicola terrestris*. It is fitting that along this stretch of the canal there still lives a community of these shy creatures, one of only five colonies identified in a survey of all the waterways in the city of Oxford in 1997.

To the west of the canal at this point is **Hook Meadow**, another Site of Special Scientific Interest. Described technically as 'unimproved neutral meadow', it is a piece of marshy grassland now rare in the Oxford area. Marsh marigolds grow here, and ragged robin and meadowsweet; waterfowl such as snipe and jack snipe are attracted to the site in wintertime. Fred Chamberlain, in his 'Recollections of Wolvercote as it was in 1910', recorded that "On Port Meadow a budding aeronaut named Gooden tried out his aeroplane, which local people called 'The Grasshopper', for it hardly ever left the ground for more than a few yards, and he had his hangars in Hook Meadow, by the railway."

'The Radiators'
Continuing south down the canal, we come to bridge 239A. **'The electric bridge'**, as it is known locally, was built in 1930 to link two halves of the Osberton Radiators factory (sites owned at the time of writing by Unipart, the parent company of Oxford Automotive Components). Uniquely for the Oxford Canal, it is power-operated. Jack and Rose Skinner regularly delivered coal

to 'The Radiators' from Bedworth and Griff collieries on the Coventry coalfield. In the 1940s Barlow's, the carrying company, paid them 3/9d per ton, which amounted to about £6 for a full load. The round trip took two weeks, and they were not paid for the week in which they returned empty. (Jack: *"It was a hard life. We used to work 16 or 17 hours a day, six or seven days a week. Many's the time me and her have set off before dawn and finished in the dark. The women had it hardest, I reckon"* ... Rose: *"We used to eat as we went along — and I used to cook as we went along an' all! Cooking with one hand and steering with the other. And the little ones*

Rose Skinner (wielding the shovel) and Jean Humphries (holding the barrow steady), unloading coal at Juxon Street wharf in Jericho, 1956.

Copyright: Oxfordshire County Council Photographic Archive

[she had four children] *playing in the boat's bottom when it was empty, or tied to the slide* [hatch] *when we were loaded."*) Although coal was their staple cargo, the Skinners also carried timber, copper, and steel. During the last war, Jack even transported a top-priority supply of nitroglycerine, which he and his mate delivered from Brentford to Birmingham up the Grand Union Canal, through 153 locks. (*"We did it in 63 hours, without stopping — kept going through the night, with a paraffin lamp on the front of the boat. That put years on me, that did! When we got to the other end, there were chaps all dressed in green fireproof stuff, with gloves and helmets. They said there was enough in one of those bottles to blow up Birnigum with!"*)

Frog Lane

There is no known date for the construction of bridge number 239, the lethally heavy **metal lift bridge at the end of Frenchay Road**, which killed one of the ten Chappell children from nearby Hayfield Road some time around 1900. A wooden version of it must have been constructed in the earliest days of the canal, to carry an ancient right of way known in the 14th century as Wycroft Lane, and now called **Frog Lane**.

Frog Lane leads due west towards Port Meadow, along the edge of **the Trap Grounds Reed Bed**, a Site of Local Importance for Nature Conservation. This is Oxford's only known breeding site for the elusive water rail; it is also host to the largest colony of breeding reed warblers in the city, and the county's only recorded population of the spider *Nesticus cellulanus*. Foxes saunter along Frog Lane in broad daylight, and muntjak deer can be glimpsed here in the twilight of summer evenings. Overhead in the big willows, woodpeckers and treecreepers build their nests in the spring.

Returning to the canal along Frog Lane, one might spare a thought for 'Little Mush', a solitary man who lived here in a shed in the 1930s. Isolated from the world by a severe speech impediment, he had a rifle and a spiteful goose (*"to ward off the Social"*, according to local people who remember him). He used to pick coals from the railway line, and was always filthy. (*"Once his sister persuaded him to go and live with her in Reading, but she made him have a bath, so he came back the next day."*) In another shed somewhere in this vicinity lived 'Paraffin Liz', reputed once to have been the Librarian of Somerville College. In the 1920s and 1930s she made a living by giving riding lessons to children on Port Meadow (allegedly using horses that did not belong to her). According to local legend, *"she always rode bare-back. She was a queer old soul, as skinny as a herring. She wore men's boots, and string for a belt, and she had dinner in the Randolph Hotel every night."*

Opposite the end of Frog Lane there used to be a small wharf, where the electricity sub-station is now. Known as Hambridge's Wharf (although it was leased by the Corporation of Oxford from 1900 to 1925), it sold coal and firewood to local householders. Many generations of the extensive Hambridge

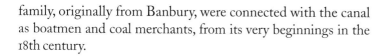
family, originally from Banbury, were connected with the canal as boatmen and coal merchants, from its very beginnings in the 18th century.

 ## Hayfield Wharf

South of Hambridge's on the east bank are the long, neat gardens of the householders in Hayfield Road (who used to have to render one shilling each as annual payment to the Canal Company for the use of the bank). Before these houses were built in 1886, there were some old cottages, home in the 1840s to a small community of boat-builders, among whom were John Pebody and his wife Ann, with their sons Oliver and Caleb. The Pebody family was well known along the whole length of the Oxford Canal, from Braunston and Banbury down to Oxford.

The canal has always played a large part in the lives of the Hayfield Road community. Until the 1950s it was clean enough for the children to swim in, and Mrs Jessie Harding, born in Hayfield Road in 1910 and resident there all her life, remembered, *"You could see the bottom from the drawbridge to Aristotle Lane, and it was full of roach and perch. We used to fish for 'red soldiers' [perch?] with a bent pin and a bit of string."* Mrs Doris Thicke, another long-time resident, recalled:

> *"The canal people were very friendly. The same families would travel up and down the canal all year. I remember the Skinners and the Beauchamps. They all waved when they passed the end of our garden. The men used to throw their boots into the garden of number 3, for Tommy Tombs to mend them. They would collect them on the way back up. The boats had glistening brasses, and clothes hung out to dry as white as milk. Those women were tough! They wore hob-nailed boots, and unloaded coal just like the men. But they put on clean aprons and caps to visit Dolly's Hut* [The Anchor public house in Hayfield Road, opposite the wharf]. *They couldn't read or write: they just signed with a cross."*

The Anchor was originally a hostelry known as Heyfield's Hutt, named after the landlord who presided over it for many

years and died there at the age of 90 in 1778. In his time, the inn seems to have had a rather dubious reputation. We learn from *Jackson's Oxford Journal* of 25 February 1764 of a game of cards in which the eminent Dr Webb, a tooth-drawer, blood-letter, and wig-maker, lost 44 guineas and the mortgage deeds of two houses in St Thomas's. Although the inn was renamed as The Anchor in the 1840s, it was universally known until quite recently as Dolly's Hut, taking the name from another landlord, William Dolley, who presided there for a quarter of a century from 1852. The pub was a favourite with boatpeople, and it is tempting to imagine Rose Skinner's grandfather, Alfred Hone senior, singing in the snug in the 1890s:

> "He could play the squeezebox, and dance and sing, all at the same time. He had a clear true whistle too, and a rattle of wooden bobbins. 'Shake them bobbins!' he used to sing. It was a song the old boat-chaps used to sing to make their 'orses get a move on."

(These recollections of Alfred Hone were recorded by Sheila Stewart in *Ramlin Rose: The Boatwoman's Story*, a novel drawn from the composite experiences of true-life boatwomen, including Rose Skinner.)

Hayfield Wharf (illustrated opposite) was an important feature of the Oxford Canal from its earliest days. *Jackson's Journal* recorded on 3 October 1789:

> The Oxford Canal being finished and opened at the wharf at Hayfields Hutt, within a quarter of a mile of Oxford, the best coals are sold at the following prices: Oakthorpe coals, 1s 5d. per cwt; Warwickshire 1s 2d per cwt; Staffordshire coke per ton, £1 4s. 9d.

Coal merchants came long distances with horse-drawn carts to take deliveries from the wharf, which was well equipped with a weighing office and stables for the boatmen's horses and mules. (Other stables could be rented across the road next to The Anchor, on the site of the present Aladdin Garage, or the other side of Aristotle Bridge in the yard of the last house in Kingston Road.) On this wharf in the 1870s there was a mission room, which was supported by the congregation of the church of St Philip and St James in Leckford Road. Sunday afternoon services were

Opposite:
Hayfield Wharf, c. 1890. The 1891 census suggests the following identifications (from right): Frank Restall, the owner; Jane Johnson and her husband Thomas, coal merchant, who lived on the wharf in Navigation House (out of the picture); and their maid Sarah Simmonds. The two boys in the centre are probably Ernest and Leonard Tuffrey, also living at Navigation House. The well-scrubbed narrowboats appear to be crewed by one man and five women. Note their traditional bonnets and spotless aprons.

Copyright: Oxfordshire County Council Photographic Archive

held here, presumably for the benefit of the boatpeople (for whose welfare and morals there was much concern in Victorian society). The Women's Guild paid half the rent, and several of the men from this prosperous, philanthropic congregation taught at a night school held there during the winter months. The mission room was pulled down in 1883.

Some time around 1875, a tall brick building called Navigation House was built on the wharf. Here lived Thomas Johnson, described in the Oxford Directory as a 'coal and manure merchant and beer retailer'. He was assisted by his son-in-law, Anthony Harris (son of the landlord of The Anchor). On wash-days in the 1920s, Mrs Mary Harris, wife of Albert Harris, the foreman on the wharf, would cook faggots and peas on her kitchen range, and the women of Hayfield Road would send their children down the street with basins to fetch dinner for the family. The boys of Hayfield Road could earn a few pence by helping to groom and feed the boatmen's horses after school. The wharf closed down in the early 1950s, but Navigation House lingered on until the 1960s, when it was demolished to make way for the offices of Midland Builders (now used by Oxford Illustrators).

Aristotle Lane to Lucy's Ironworks

Bridge 240, the hump-backed brick bridge at Hayfield Wharf, is a Grade II listed construction, carrying an ancient right of way to Port Meadow, known originally as 'the lower way to Wolvercote' (according to Herbert Hurst, the author of *Oxford Topography* in 1899, quoting from Leonard Hutten's *Dissertation on the Antiquities of Oxford* of 1625). Until 1841, when a bridge was built over the canal nearer to the city at Walton Well Lane, Aristotle Lane was the chief entrance on to the Meadow from the east.

The right of way was much disputed in the Middle Ages by the city authorities and the Abbess of Godstow, who owned the surrounding land. Eventually, to keep an eye on the lane and stop her blocking it, the Council built a house at the eastern end, to accommodate 'the reeve's man'. According to the *Victoria County History*, a herdsman's house, built at the gate to the Lane in 1582, was used in 1603 and 1608 to house plague victims; it finally fell down in 1629.

On 3 June 1644, King Charles I slipped out of Oxford by night, marching north with 6,000 men up the line of what is now Kingston Road, under the shadow of the tree-crowned gravel bank, 30 feet high, which (according to Hurst) in those days ran along its length. They escaped along Aristotle Lane, to cross Port Meadow and make a dash for the West Country.

The lane acquired its name from Aristotle's Well, sited in what is now the cellar of the house on the corner of Kingston Road and the Lane. On this site in the late 12th century lived a Norman knight, Brooman le Riche. The 17th-century diarist Anthony Wood recorded that in his day the well was a favourite haunt of scholars, walking out from Oxford in summer (perhaps from Plato's Well, at the southern end of what is now Walton Street?). By 1718, according to the journal of the contemporary local historian Thomas Hearne, there was a house of refreshment near the well, and it is tempting to suppose that he meant a cottage on the site of the present Anchor which appears on Benjamin Cole's map of Port Meadow, published in 1720.

It was over Aristotle Bridge between 1849 and 1852 that thousands of tons of gravel were taken by tramway from Cabbage Hill, later to become Kingston Road, and Lark Hill, later to become Chalfont Road. The gravel was used for the embankment of the Great Western Railway, which was constructed parallel to the canal, about 300 yards to the west. Its removal cleared the way for the eventual development of this area of North Oxford. Today the only remnant of the gravel bank forms the western boundary of St Margaret's churchyard in Kingston Road.

It was under Aristotle Bridge that the Skinners' boat *Redshank*, towing the butty *Greenshank*, got stuck in 1954 or 1955. By the mid-1950s the canal, which had been losing trade to the road hauliers since the war, was no longer being dredged every Whit Monday and was silting up and becoming choked with weeds. There was talk of closing it. Public feeling against the closure was demonstrated at a protest meeting held in Oxford Town

Hall on 3 June 1955, chaired by the poet John Betjeman. By this time, Jack and Rose were working for Willow Wren, a small independent carrying company formed in 1953 with some surplus boats bought from British Waterways. Jack recalls the epic journey which he and Rose undertook, to prove that the canal was still navigable:

> *"Me and her and Willow Wren put our heads together and decided the best way to save the canal was to prove that it could still carry traffic. So we brought 50 tons of coal from Nuneaton to Juxon's wharf for Morrell's Brewery. We did all right till we got to Dolly's Hut. The water there was very shallow, because the kids had thrown rubbish into it. We had to bowhaul the butty through* [drag it along with a rope from the towpath], *but we did it!"*

Ten years later, Jack saved the canal from closure a second time. Barbara Castle, the Minister of Transport, was minded to close it down and fill it in. Jack was asked to take her on a fact-finding trip along a stretch farther north, near Thrupp. He took the precaution of going out the night before and opening all the lock paddles, to give the impression that there was more water in the near-derelict canal than there actually was. *"She never knew the difference — and it done the trick"*, he recalled with pride. Mrs Castle decided to up-grade the canal and invest in its conservation as a 'recreational and amenity waterway'. Everyone who now enjoys fishing in the canal, or cruising on it, or walking along it should remember with gratitude Jack Skinner and the trick he played on the Minister of Transport.

The Missing Bridge

Sharp-eyed walkers along the towpath will have noticed that Aristotle Bridge is numbered 240, and the next bridge south, at Walton Well Road, is number 242. What happened to 241? It is there in the report of the Chain Survey undertaken by the Canal Company in 1840 (one of a series recording every bridge, lock, and other notable structure along the 77-mile length of the canal). Ten chains (one-eighth of a mile) from 'Hayfields Hut Bridge' was 'the Workhouse Bridge': just south of where the builder's yard of Hutchins and Green in **Southmoor Road** now fronts the canal on the east bank. The stone footings of the bridge are still in the water and can be seen from the towpath. A photograph taken in 1868, preserved in the Bodleian Library, shows it as a timber drawbridge, similar in design to the bridge near St Edward's School, but more rustic in its construction. The 1876 Ordnance Survey map shows it clearly, but there is no associated structure nearby, nor any track leading to it or away from it. It is aligned with 'Farndon Place' (now Farndon Road), down which presumably livestock was driven, through fields and across the canal for grazing. The bridge was probably demolished in 1882, when the houses at the north end of Southmoor Road were built.

Bridge 241, 'The Workhouse Bridge', seen from the south: a drawing by Jenny Modéer, based on a photograph of 1868 in the Bodleian Library. The sloping fields on the right are now the gardens of Kingston Road. Aristotle Bridge is seen in the background.

But why was it called 'Workhouse Bridge'? Perhaps it was associated with the City Workhouse established on Rats and Mice Hill (now Wellington Square) in 1771. *Jackson's Oxford Journal* of 10 February 1849 lamented the fact that this establishment was too small to provide outdoor productive work for the training of inmates in useful skills. Was Bridge 241 an early example of a job-creation scheme? Alternatively, it might have been associated with St Thomas's Poorhouse and Workhouse, which in the late 18th century stood on the south side of Hythe Bridge Street — next to The Nag's Head, where much canal business was transacted. It might be surmised that someone — perhaps the enterprising Daniel Harris, of whom more below (see 'Sheepwash Channel') — won the tender for the job by using cheap labour from the workhouse.

A third possible explanation for the name 'Workhouse Bridge' is suggested by the fact that for many years until 1865, according to the *Victoria County History*, the Oxford Board of Guardians ran a small mixed farm, presumably employing workhouse inmates, on land on the east bank, where now the gardens of Southmoor Road slope down to the water. This area, labelled 'Pepper Hills' on an enclosure map of 1769, was sufficiently isolated from the city for a cholera hospital and dispensary to be erected here after the Radcliffe Infirmary refused to admit victims during the terrible 22-week epidemic of 1832. (The location was somewhat ironic, given the popular belief at the time that cholera was spread from town to town by canal boats and their crews.)

Such harsh realities were not in the mind of the poet James Elroy Flecker, who may have been thinking of this stretch of water when he composed his poem 'Oxford Canal' in the early years of the 20th century:

When you have wearied of the valiant spires of this County Town ...
Of its red motors and lumbering trams, and self-sufficient people,
I will take you walking with me to a place you have not seen —
Half town and half country — the land of the Canal ...

"Half town and half country" describes it very well. An Oxford guidebook, published by Ward, Lock & Co. in 1898, describes the canal as presenting "an arcadian scene of pastoral beauty". Mrs Sylvia Johnson, who was born in **Kingston Road**, alongside the canal, in 1908, and lived there all her life, remembered this stretch of the Cut as far more rural than it is now: *"There was much more wildlife in the old days — water voles, grass-snakes, and dab-chicks. I saw an otter in the Isis from Port Meadow once, and you could hear bitterns by the river."* Mrs Johnson recalled that the canal seemed to freeze more often in the old days. She remembered skating to work in the town centre, and the arrival of the steel boat drawn by six horses, carrying eight men on each side, rocking the boat from side to side to break the ice.

Lucy's Ironworks

The pleasantly rural stretch of water at the back of Kingston and Southmoor Roads ends abruptly in dank gloom under **bridge 242**, which carries Walton Well Road to Port Meadow; beyond it on the east bank is the burning fiery furnace of **Lucy's Eagle Ironworks** — a stark reminder of the industrial origins of the canal system. The firm was founded in 1812, or perhaps earlier, by William Carter, who traded from his shop in the High Street as an "ironmonger, hardwareman, brazier, and tinplate worker". (The foundry acquired the name 'Eagle' under Carter's successor, Charles Grafton; William Lucy took over the firm in the 1860s, and it still thrives under his name.)

The foundry moved to Jericho in 1825 from Summertown, north of Oxford. The attractions of the canal-side site must have been obvious: coal and raw materials could be delivered direct to the company's own wharf, and its finished products — iron railings, lamp-posts, agricultural tools — could be taken away by water. An article in *The Clarendonian* of 1923, recalling Walton Manor in the 1860s, describes a now-vanished scene on the edge of the present works:

> ... a Dock, parallel with the Canal, and covered in by a roof on wooden supports, but open at the sides; here boats were both built and repaired. The road to Port Meadow led over the canal by a drawbridge, and over the two railway lines by a level crossing.

There is now no trace of this boatyard; the lift bridge has been replaced by a heavy, graceless brick bridge, and the level crossing by an iron railway bridge, uncompromising in its ugliness.

On the west bank of the canal below Walton Well bridge, a brick wall now hides part of Lucy's operations. This is remembered by Ted Harris, a resident of Jericho, as Johnson's Field, a sloping piece of grassy meadowland full of wild flowers. He recalled playing there as a child in the 1940s.

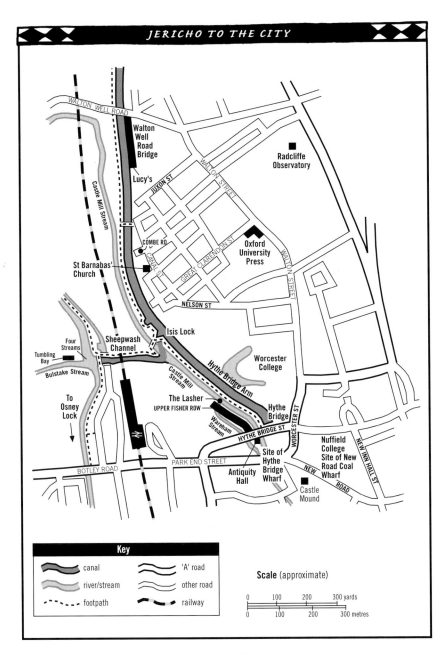

Key

canal		'A' road	
river/stream		other road	
footpath		railway	

Scale (approximate)

0   100   200   300 yards

0   100   200   300 metres

Jericho

Where Lucy's wall ends, a stream can be seen running parallel to the canal on the west side. This was the main course of the Thames up to the end of the 18th century. It flows next to the canal all the way into the city, where it formerly powered the mill attached to Oxford Castle, and is therefore known as Castle Mill Stream.

On the east bank is the site of Juxon Street Wharf. This was the first of a series of the Canal Company's wharves stretching down to Worcester College. A Company map of 1811 shows these plots as open fields, and an 1850 map by Robert Hoggar is little different: new housing is shown only in the vicinity of the Oxford University Press building, which was completed in 1832. By the end of the century the fields (illustrated overleaf) had vanished. The 1876 Ordnance Survey map shows canalside yards with specific areas for coal, stone, and timber. In 1927, when the Company decided to sell its central wharves at Hythe Bridge and New Road, these Jericho wharves were considered to be "ample alternative accommodation ... for delivery and stacking of all goods carried on the Canal". Not that many people in Oxford would have noticed. University dons had been prominent among the Company's early shareholders, but this initial enthusiasm gradually waned. After the profitable early years, one gets the impression that the canal's workmanlike intrusion into Oxford's collegiate grandeur was met with increasingly snobbish disdain.

The enduring indifference of the public is illustrated in an incident from the book *Idle Women*, which tells the story of an all-women boatcrew recruited by the Ministry of Labour during the second world war. In it, Susan Woolfit records that having moored up "somewhere behind Worcester College" on their first trip to Oxford, they lost their bearings during an excursion into the city, and found little assistance from local inhabitants, who "seemed to be entirely ignorant of the presence of a canal in the city". Jack and Rose Skinner were generous in their praise of these all-women crews, 'trainees' as they were known. Jack

thought they were *"better than all the men put together"*, partly because they were more willing to listen to advice — although they fell in the Skinners' esteem because of their refusal to dress up on the rare occasions when they socialised together. The boatpeople were always careful to look smart at public events, and were embarrassed by the scruffy working clothes which the middle-class trainees chose to wear.

The footbridge over the canal at the southern end of Lucy's wall was dubbed "a bridge to nowhere" when it was erected in 1972 — indicative of the low esteem in which this practically forgotten waterway was held even then. Other choice descriptions from the local press at about this time included "Oxford's slum canal", "a civic disgrace", and "total squalor".

By the mid-1980s a large number of residential boats had accumulated on the stretch of canal from Jericho northwards. These boats were the cause of some concern to the authorities, and a well-publicised dispute over mooring rights ensued. In 1985 a councillor was quoted as saying, *"We do not want a boat city in Oxford, and are determined that this little flotilla is going to have to sail on."* The British Waterways Board was equally uncompromising, seemingly unable or unwilling to offer any better solution than to threaten the boat dwellers with eviction and confiscation of their vessels.

Local residents tended to side with the boaters. In 1985 an Inland Waterways Association spokesperson had said of the canal, *"People tell us that they never walk along there because it's so nasty"*. Yet by 1987 a letter from the Jericho Residents' Association printed in the *Oxford Times* was saying that the presence of the boats *"positively increases the amenity value and security of the canal bank in our area. They have turned an often dangerous towpath into an area integrated with Jericho."* This sentiment shows a certain continuity. Relations between the working boatpeople and bankside residents seem always to have been good — they were to some extent mutually dependent, after all — and the prejudices against boatpeople have tended to emanate from much further afield. Eventually the authorities too softened their attitude. The 'saga of the Oxford boatpeople' as it became known had gained national notoriety (and even

Opposite:
Jericho viewed from the west, *c.* 1835, showing three prominent buildings: the Radcliffe Observatory (far left), Jericho House (now the Jericho Tavern), and Oxford University Press (far right). The latter was completed in 1832, and the absence of housing around the Press suggests that this somewhat idealised view from the canal towpath was drawn very soon after. The same view today would place St Barnabas' Church somewhere near the copse of trees in the centre of the picture.

Copyright: Oxfordshire County Council Photographic Archive

international, with the coverage of a Soviet film crew on the track of an unacceptable facet of capitalism!) and four years after it had begun, the dispute was partially resolved with the establishment of permanent moorings at Hythe Bridge Arm in 1989. The perseverance of the floating population is to be admired, but credit is also due to those in authority, who adjusted their position to such an extent that today we see British Waterways and the City Council energetically seeking new residential mooring sites.

Oxford has an unusually high concentration of residential boats. It could be said that these boat dwellers represent the perpetuation of the working boatpeople's traditional life-styles, in that their boats are year-round homes. Meanwhile, the canal's commercial continuity — aside from the handful of working boats which still transport freight, mostly coal, around the system — is provided by holiday hire boats. These are plentiful today, but in 1957 the Oxford Canal Association noted the four hotel-boat companies and one hire-boat operator then on the southern Oxford Canal as a "compara-tively recent innovation". Denis Wise, whose familiarity with the canal in Jericho stretches back more than four decades, recalled one horse-drawn boat which operated passenger trips from Hythe Bridge Street to Wolvercote and Thrupp around 1960. The owners had installed bus seats, charging 10s 6d return, including refreshments. It seems likely that this boat was *Gertrude*, Jack and Rose Skinner's first butty. In an article for the *Oxford Times*, Kingsley Belsten said it was used for just such a purpose in 1960, making it the last horse-drawn boat on the Oxford Canal. (Jack's uncle, Joe, had the distinction of running the last horse-drawn freight boat.) The horse fell into Isis Lock on one occasion, according to Denis, and had to be rescued by the Fire Brigade!

The canal's transition from a working environment to a largely leisure-based resource has been relatively sudden. The 1990s saw another major change, this time in the attitude of the Oxford public, spurred on by the unprecedented interest of property developers in canalside land. An event organised in April 1995 by Friends of the Earth, the boating community, and

Opposite:
Passengers replacing freight in an early example of the canal's transition to the tourism and leisure trade. Pictured on Hythe Bridge Arm in 1957, the boat is thought to be *Gertrude*, Jack and Rose Skinner's first butty.

Copyright: Oxfordshire County Council Photographic Archive

nearby residents' associations highlighted the likely cumulative impact of developments then proposed for nine separate sites along the canal corridor. Over a thousand people assembled in a human chain running the full one and a half miles' length of these combined developments, and a petition signed by some 900 people asked for sensitive treatment of the sites and for traffic to be kept to a minimum. This unprecedented unity of 'boat and bank' showed clearly that appreciation of the environmental, recreational, and heritage value of the canal had spread wider than ever before.

The front page of the Oxford Mail of 3 April 1995 after an unprecedented show of public concern over intensive developments proposed for land alongside the canal. 800 demonstrators, to the authors' certain knowledge, was an underestimate.

Copyright: Oxford Mail

The Canal Ferry

Oxford's only current boat-hire company, College Cruisers, now occupies the wharves which the O.S. map of 1876 shows being used for coal and stone. The site used to be overlooked by a Canal Company property called Ferry House. According to Ted Harris, a nearby resident for some 60 years, the scullery was incorporated into the rear of the single-storey brick building used as College's office. The ferry in question was a large punt, introduced largely for the convenience of railway workers going from the new suburb of Jericho to the engine sheds, workshops and stations on the west side of Castle Mill Stream. The indent in the wharf where the ferry was berthed is still visible, just as shown in the 1876 O.S. map. It was known to Ted Harris always as Herbert's Ferry, after the occupant of Ferry House from 1897/98 to 1927, a coalmerchant called William Herbert.

The importance of the ferry grew in the 1930s when the Jericho wharves replaced the Basin as the canal's Oxford freight terminus: then it was also needed to transfer towhorses across to stables on the Jericho side. It was obviously already quite an institution, though. The Canal Company's minutes of 11 December 1928 declined a suggestion from Oxford Corporation to build a footbridge, on the basis that the ferry was quite adequately run by the tenant of their house there. The ferryman himself lived in the end house of Combe Road. Called Ferry Place for two or three years when it was first built, then

Ferry Road from 1890, this short street was renamed in 1959 after Thomas Combe, who provided the funds for the construction of **St Barnabas' Church**. The new name was needed to avoid confusion with another Ferry Road in Marston. Ted Harris remembered the residents getting quite indignant about this, because the Marston ferry had long since vanished, while the Jericho one was still very much in evidence, continuing into the 1960s according to both Ted Harris and Jack Skinner.

Ferry in the Oxford Canal

Canal Ferry and Ferry House, c.1860. The buildings and ferry are absent from Hoggar's map of 1850, but appear on the 1876 Ordnance Survey map, by which time the trees in the background had disappeared. These trees seem likely to be the same as those shown in the centre of the depiction of Jericho fields on page 22.

Copyright: Oxfordshire County Council Photographic Archive

St Barnabas' Church

Thomas Combe was manager of the Oxford University Press for many years, and also owned Wolvercote Paper Mill from 1855 till 1872. To cater for the perceived spiritual needs of the youthful and growing population around the Press, Combe commissioned the construction of St Barnabas' Church. He asked that it should be modelled on Torcello Cathedral near Venice, and that no funds should be wasted on the external appearance. The church is thought to be the original of St Silas', which Thomas Hardy incorporated into *Jude the Obscure* in 1896, while the district of Beersheba, where Jude first found lodgings, is modelled on Jericho. The church was consecrated in 1869, and the campanile erected in 1872, on land donated by the coalmerchant William Ward. Henry Ward, presumably

William's father, had established the original wharf at the end of today's Nelson Street in 1829, and provided the funds for a special floating chapel for boatmen near Hythe Bridge Street in the 1830s. Some years later another coalmerchant, William Herbert of Ferry House, evidently also had strong affiliations with St Barnabas': a plaque in this temple of high-church Anglicanism commemorates the deaths of his sons, William Percival (aged six) and Montague George (aged seven), in 1902 and 1905 respectively, and describes the Herbert boys as "bearers of the incense boat". The younger brother was almost certainly named after the greatly appreciated first vicar, Montague Noel, who remained for some 30 years. One, perhaps both, of the Herbert boys are thought to have drowned in the canal.

At the time of writing, the church is backdrop to the derelict site of a boatyard which ceased trading in the early 1990s. Of note is a dry dock, a former forge, and a small stable building — rare reminders of the canal's working heritage. The dry dock is a product of recent decades, while the forge was probably built to coincide with the Canal Company's move from the Basin, as it appears on an O.S. map for the first time in 1937. The older stables are currently the temporary offices of the cruising restaurant *Rosamund the Fair*.

Sheepwash Channel

Ted Harris remembered a second ferry crossing the canal near Nelson Street during the Second World War. This was a punt provided by the Corporation specifically to enable children from Jericho to go to Tumbling Bay, the now neglected Victorian open-air bathing place on the old main Thames navigation of Bulstake Stream.

To trace this route to Tumbling Bay, bear right across the bridge over Castle Mill Stream just before Isis Lock, and under the railway bridge — originally constructed across the Sheepwash Channel by the Oxford and Rugby Railway Co in the 1840s — to **Four Streams** at the junction with the Thames. Another ferry, a public one, used to transport people from here

to the Tumbling Bay pools (one for males, one for females) for a
fare of 1d. Nancy Sherratt, who often used to walk here from her
father's home at Hythe Bridge Wharf, had clear memories
of the ferryman in the 1920s. Known as 'Butcher' Long, he
would often give the apprehensive children forewarning of the
temperature of the water in the bathing area.

The route to Four Streams passes a second railway crossing
of the Sheepwash, **a swing bridge** built in 1851 to allow the
Buckinghamshire (later London & North West, then London,
Midland and Scottish) Railway to cross to marshalling yards
and a station on the site of the old Rewley Abbey. In 1853, a railway engine toppled into the Sheepwash, the driver having failed
to realise that the bridge had been opened for a boat to pass. The
LMS station closed for conventional passenger use in 1951, but
goods trains continued to bring in domestic coal on a regular, if
infrequent, basis. The swing bridge seems usually to have been
positioned to allow boats to pass. Ray Titcomb used to come
this way from his childhood home in Upper Fisher Row a year
or two earlier, and recalled that even when the bridge crossed
the channel, you could still wriggle underneath the tracks if
clean clothes were not a priority! Now a static Scheduled
Ancient Monument, the bridge was operating at least until 1975,
when the *Shell Book of Inland Waterways* corroborated the
memories of Ted Harris and Denis Wise by assuring the reader
that "if closed, application to the signalman or station staff will
result in the appearance of a gang of spanner-men whose func-
tion is to unbolt the tracks prior to winding the span aside". The
last coalmerchants, Taylor & Sons, moved off the Rewley
Abbey site in the mid-1990s.

The Sheepwash Channel runs from today's main Thames
at Four Streams to the confluence with Castle Mill Stream at
the southern tip of the tract of land to the west of the Stream
(known as 'Snakes' Island' to Ted Harris and his school friends).
At certain times in the past, the main river navigation through
Oxford was probably via the stretch of Castle Mill Stream flow-
ing past Fisher Row, or some parallel watercourse now altered
out of recognition. For at least part of the 17th and 18th centuries, however, it was the Sheepwash which constituted a vital

part of the navigable route. Vessels coming down the northern section of Castle Mill Stream from Medley would turn right up the Sheepwash to reach the Bulstake Stream and on eventually to join today's Thames downstream of Osney Lock.

There are suggestions that the Sheepwash might originally, or perhaps seasonally, have run westwards in contraflow to today's easterly course. Once Osney Lock had been completed in 1790 (see below), the pound of water upstream of it would inevitably have been raised, and could conceivably have caused this reversal of flow direction in the Sheepwash. The network of streams in this part of Oxford has been so much affected by man's interventions that this does seem feasible, especially given that the comparable river connection of Duke's Cut north of Wolvercote could run both lower and higher than the canal. Whatever, the Sheepwash was evidently no longer passable by the time the need for an efficient connection between canal and river was being discussed in the 1790s. In a letter written on 12 April 1793, the Reverend David Durell, who was both chairman of the Canal Company and a Thames Commissioner, described it as a branch of the river "not now in a navigable state but which might easily be rendered so". He was right. Entries in the Thames Commissioners' ledgers between 8 October 1796 and 3 December 1796 record the expenses of "Ballasting and Defining of the Sheepwash a Chanel from the Cernal warff in to the Thames Navigation Oxford" amounting to £27 10s 6d, at a cost per man per day of 2s 6d.

These were the words of John Treacher, an uneducated man from one of the branches of a family with long-established connections with the river. In 1791, he became the first of three generations of Treachers to be appointed Surveyor of the entire Thames, while the Oxford branch of the family used wealth acquired as barge owners to become influential in the local commerce and governance of Oxford. It is interesting to note Treacher's implication that the flow of the Sheepwash did indeed run *from* the canal *to* the river in 1796 — even though this was *after* the construction of Osney Lock.

Daniel Harris

Osney was one of six (of the total of twelve) Thames locks upstream of Folly Bridge to be completed in 1790/91, as the Thames Commissioners reacted a little belatedly to the new opportunities offered by the canals. The man responsible for many of these locks and a great number of other navigational improvements was Daniel Harris, the keeper of Oxford Castle Gaol from 1786 onwards. In this position he was able to provide plentiful convict labour, but he was also a surveyor, an engineer, and an architect — capacities in which he played a hugely important, yet hitherto scarcely recognised, role in the affairs of both the canal and river authorities.

In his earlier years Harris had been a journeyman carpenter, and one gets the impression that despite his subsequent mastery of architectural and engineering skills, and eminent position at the prison, he was often hampered by his lowly origins. Before any recorded involvement with the waterways, in 1786, he had attracted considerable ridicule as the subject of a vitriolic and very public drawing which had been pinned on the prison gates. It turned out to have been commissioned by Harris' immediate superior as an act of petty revenge. Ultimately, the culprit was dismissed and Harris promoted in his stead to the position of Keeper of the Gaol — although not without some damage to his reputation, one can imagine, since the title of the caricature, 'Daniel Damnable', and the circumstances leading to its creation, seem indicative of wider animosity. Not long after, in 1791, Harris was again involved in controversy, by biasing public opinion against a well-known murder suspect in advance of the trial and then being implicated in certain payments to the principal witness.

If these incidents in connection with Harris' role as an influential public servant raise doubts about his character, there can be little question about his wide-ranging talents and energy in respect of the fortunes of waterborne transport in the Oxford area. His first recorded involvement on the Thames occurred in 1789, when he was commissioned to build Osney Lock. This was one of several such associations with the river which apparently attracted widespread public sarcasm — although it is unclear whether this was due to Harris' background, his lack of formal engineering skills, the use of convicts, his suspect public persona, or a combination of all these. Whatever the reasons, the Thames Commissioners stuck with him, and charged him with repairing bridges and weirs, making gates, creating new channels and towpaths, and ballasting over a full 30 miles of river stretching from Rushey to Nuneham. A letter-cum-report written by him at the Castle on 29 January 1795 lists these undertakings in full. Among them is included the means to control the flow to both the Bulstake Stream and the Sheepwash: "At the four streams a Weir is ready to be fixed. At the Sheepwash a bridge 50' long and Gates is fixed." In the second volume of *The Thames Highway*, Fred S Thacker's authoritative 1920 survey of navigation on the Thames, the bridge he alludes to here as "formerly of timber, with three openings; exceedingly troublesome to the barges on account of the abrupt turn under it" is presumably the self-same one, or at least a later adaptation of it. Today **a single-span iron footbridge** crosses the Sheepwash at Four Streams. This bridge was built in 1866, and, in combination with the broader one of 1851 which crosses Castle Mill Stream from Isis Lock, was the means by which railway employees using the ferry from Jericho could make their daily journeys to work. These bridges were also undoubtedly advantageous for the boathandlers, saving their tow-horses a long detour via Hythe Bridge Street and Botley Road. Indeed, if the railway authorities are to be believed, the bridge over Castle Mill Stream was built expressly for this purpose, "exclusively for the use of boathorses passing from the Canal to the River towpath". The steeply curving 1866 bridge still exhibits struts designed to assist the horses' footing.

For the Canal Company, Harris negotiated numerous land and property purchases in what appears to have been an unofficial agency role. Of note he designed the Company's original headquarters of Wyaston House in New Inn Hall Street, and provided the labour for the construction of **Isis Lock** and various other works on the canal.

Isis Lock to Hythe Bridge Street

Isis Lock

This picturesque lock, marking the junction of the canal and river, has suffered a sinister, unsavoury reputation belying the tranquillity of its present-day setting. Today Isis Lock is a narrow one, that is, seven feet wide, the breadth which distinguishes a narrowboat from a barge, but it was originally designed specifically to allow river barges access to the central wharves of the Basin. The location was decided only after the feasibility of the **Sheepwash Channel** had been confirmed as a means of navigation. The Company's minutes of 20 August 1793 resolved to build a chamber lock "at the most convenient place near the Oxford Wharf to communicate with the River Thames, and that Mr Daniel Harris of the castle be employed to build same".

This new lock — referred to in the Canal Company's ledgers simply as 'Oxford Lock' — was evidently well underway by the beginning of 1795, since Harris was paid various sums from then on, with the final settlement of the balance of his specific Oxford Lock account being made in March 1797. At the same time, the Company purchased several river barges between 1793 and 1802, specifically for conveying goods to and from London on the Thames. By 1800, with trade expanding, they resolved to widen the arch of the bridge between their terminal wharves at Hythe Bridge and New Road "so as to admit Thames barges into the new wharf".

When and why Isis Lock was narrowed remains something of a mystery. In an authoritative canal map of 1833 it is still labelled as a "barge lock", and while Robert Hoggar's 1850 map shows it as narrow, there is no way of knowing how accurately he surveyed structures lying outside the city's built-up area. Certainly, it is possible that Hoggar, like so many others before and after him, thought better of the walk down a muddy, lonely towpath, and made an educated guess! It is indicative, perhaps, that the nearby Worcester College was known jocularly as 'Botany Bay' at exactly this time, on account of its remoteness. All that can be said with certainty is that the lock was narrow by 1876, conclusively shown as such in the O.S. map of that year.

In his 1898 novel *The Strange Adventures of a Houseboat*, William Black describes the lock as "a little toy-box kind of a basin". The magazine serialisation of this book carried an illustration of the lock which suggests that the splendid iron bridge is a 20th century addition, even though its fabrication date may well be rather earlier. Certainly a note in the 1840 Canal Company Chain Survey book refers to the bridge here being wooden at that time.

Isis Lock Bridge, 1998. The lock was built in 1796, and reduced in width some 50 years later. It is still often referred to by the local name of 'Louse'. In the background is the bridge over Castle Mill Stream, leading to the Sheepwash Channel. It was built in 1851 to give towhorses access to the Thames and enable railway employees from Jericho to get to work.

Copyright: Mark Davies

The importance of the Oxford Canal as part of the shortest water route from the Midlands to London had been shortlived. As early as 1805 the wider, much more direct, Grand Union Canal deprived it of this claim, and, with the increasing competition of road and rail, a significant fall in river trade was almost inevitable. No doubt Isis Lock was made narrower to reduce water usage. In retrospect this seems symbolic: an attempt to stem the outflow of lifeblood from a transport system which was failing to match its competition. Or a case of 'closing the lockgate after the tow-horse has bolted' perhaps! Whatever, Isis Lock remains now as ever a significant gateway to a canal system which extended to 3,750 miles at its peak around 1840 and even today comprises some 2,000 miles in a network reaching north of York.

Nowadays the name Isis Lock enjoys wide usage, but all older residents and boaters have always known it as Louse Lock, to the extent that Della James, born and raised in Upper Fisher Row, said she *"didn't know it was called anything else"*. British Waterways' archives show Isis as *their* name for the lock at least as early as 1912, but the Oxford Canal Association was still referring to the Thames backwater (actually Castle Mill Stream) by Isis Lock as "Louse stream" in 1957, and the *Shell Book of Inland Waterways* proffers Louse as the name as late as 1975, adding that it was then "more politely" known as Isis. Quite why the Canal Company's original name of Oxford Lock came to be replaced by the derogatory Louse remains unclear, but there is perhaps no need to look much further than the prisoners' involvement in its construction. Daniel Harris' reputation probably didn't help, and, as the closest of 'his' locks to the city, Isis would have been more likely than the Thames locks to acquire a colloquial rather than official name. Subsequently, the lock's exclusive use by boatpeople, mistakenly assumed to be dirty and insanitary, could easily have perpetuated the idea. Sheila Stewart's reference in *Ramlin Rose* to the frequency with which the boatpeople were referred to as "Dirty boatees! Lousy boatees!" is indicative.

Ray Titcomb always remembered Isis Lock as a "dismal" sort of place, to which his mother forbade him to go — ineffectively, of course, since leaping the lock was considered a rite of passage to gang membership in his schooldays. Over time it has acquired a reputation as a suicide spot — with Jan Morris suggesting that "its steep sides rule out a change of mind" in her 1965 book *Oxford* — although substantiation of this often repeated, widely believed claim remains elusive. Undoubtedly the lock has been the scene of many drownings, but these appear usually to have been accidents, the victims being the drunks and ne'er-do-wells who frequented the lock for many decades. Residential boaters on the Hythe Bridge Arm remember an individual known simply as 'Chris under the bridge' in the early 1990s. He was reputed to have lived at Isis Lock for some 15 years!

'Chris' moved on of his own free will, but many others have been less fortunate. Ray Titcomb recalled the frequency with which drowned corpses were carried along the towpath opposite his childhood home in **Upper Fisher Row**. Colin Tustin, his brother-in-law, said it was much the same when his family moved to the Row in 1953, remembering that *"in the first 10 or 12 years after we moved here there was at least one drowning a year"*. Ted Harris also remembered *"ever such a lot of people drowning"*. They included a homeless Scotsman some 30 years ago, who was identified eventually through a Glasgow laundry mark on his shirt. The toll of drownings in the vicinity, whether accidental or self-initiated, has included at least two in the late 1990s, and had begun before the lock was even in use: a verdict of lunacy was passed on a butler of Wadham College in 1795, for instance, who was "found drowned in the Mill Stream opposite the Canal Wharf in the Fisher Row".

There have been cases of assault too. Ted Harris remembered that a local man was nearly fatally beaten by American servicemen during the war, and that all the trees were cut down in the 1950s after a spate of attacks on women. Today's tree cover is the result of extensive replanting in the mid-1970s.

All in all, then, it is perhaps no surprise that the Lock's derogatory name of Louse, and a corresponding public odium, should have persisted so long — although it is interesting that Nancy Sherratt and her sisters entertained no such feelings, thinking of it always as a "lovely" place. Having a wharfinger for a father made them perceive the canal differently, seeing it, and its associated structures and characters, as comforting lifelines rather than alien threats.

Exactly as the presence of residential boats in Jericho had done in the 1980s, the opening of permanent moorings along **Hythe Bridge Arm** in 1989 gave pedestrians a new confidence. In contrast to its 'lousy' past, Isis Lock now attracts the admiration of many. Meanwhile, new housing has sprung up to the west of Castle Mill Stream, and a bridge built over the **Sheepwash Channel** in 1998 has allowed cars into a vicinity previously the haunt of shepherds (one can only assume!) and boats, and horses, and pedestrians, and then trains. These recent changes have altered the nature of a locality which had remained peculiarly unaffected by urban Oxford throughout the city's history. There is a double irony in this. For generations the reputation of the working boatpeople seems certain to have played its part in deterring the public from frequenting the lock, yet now the presence of boats — residential this time — provides a reassurance and interest for thousands of visitors a year.

Hythe Bridge Arm

The canal which had been started near Coventry in 1769 reached central Oxford at the very end of 1789. To complete the final section, a strip of land was purchased from Worcester College to extend the cut via what is now known as Hythe Bridge Arm to the central wharves at the Basin.

The purchase from Worcester College was completed on 16 July 1788. If the College resented giving up its river bank, it is not recorded. Indeed, under the Parliamentary Acts which authorised all canal building, they had little option. As a concession, the Canal Company agreed to continue a side cut in order to provide the "Provost, Fellows and Scholars with a passage for a boat into the said Canal and from thence into the Thames and Isis from time to time and at all times hereafter without paying any thing for the same". Many years later, when the Company was cutting its losses by selling up its central holdings in 1937, "two roods and 28 perches" (a rood being equal to 40 perches, or a quarter of an acre) of Worcester's former land running parallel to the canal was sold back to the college for £500.

The Arm was deliberately terminated at Hythe Bridge during the 1940s, and by the mid-1970s this stagnant dead-end had little to commend it. One local newspaper summed it up as a "stinking ditch full of weeds, rubbish and empty bottles thrown in by local layabout alcoholics", and even the Oxford Civic Society and Oxford Preservation Trust could then see no better potential for it than infilling as a public open space. It is thanks to the efforts of volunteers from the Inland Waterways Association that it remains in use, sustaining the attractive notion that the Basin beyond Hythe Bridge might one day be reinstated as the canal's natural terminus. Appropriately, the boats using the Arm occasionally include one or two of the kind which were passing here 200 years ago: every winter, at least one boat and butty deliver coal to the residential boats here — and yes, just as when the canal first opened, the boat-delivered prices are cheaper than the local competition!

The contrast between the narrowboats and the grand Worcester College buildings makes it easy to imagine a history of friction between the erudite scholars of Worcester and the illiterate working boatpeople. The personal recollections of Jack Skinner suggest otherwise, though — by the mid 20th century, at least. According to him, there was a mutual respect between these two very different sections of society, and he also perceived nothing but acceptance from the city's shopkeepers, even if he was sometimes *"black as a crow"* from coaldust!

Relations between Worcester College and the Canal Company certainly did have their tense moments though. A very long-running dispute about the detrimental effect of the canal on the drainage of Worcester's fields was finally resolved in 1913, in favour of the College. Prior to construction of the canal, a stream from Walton Well had carried all the drainage from the north through Worcester's meadows and then into Castle Mill Stream. Because the new canal cut off this natural drainage, the Company agreed to construct a wooden culvert to run under both the canal and Castle Mill Stream to the Wareham Stream. From the 1840s, the culvert having worked well for about 50 years, Worcester's meadows became flooded with great frequency. This led the College to import tens of thousands of tons of soil to raise the level of its fields, and the Company to attempt some repairs. A comment added to the 1840 Chain Survey Book states: "wooden trunk repaired at the College end and trunk built up to the surface in brick work — and trunk under River repaired at Michaelmas 1851". It took until 1913, though, when the Company's obligation was established in law, before truly effective measures were taken — so effective in fact that they seem likely to have caused the demise of Plato's Well, which lay within Worcester's grounds near Hythe Bridge Street. This ancient water source was the last in a sequence of springs — including those at Aristotle Lane and Walton Well — emanating from the gravel terrace which paralleled the canal. It had been described by Herbert Hurst as "beautiful" and "bountiful" as late as 1899.

Upper Fisher Row

The culvert from the College still exists, stretching to what is known as the **Lasher** at the northern end of Upper Fisher Row. A lasher, as mentioned in relation to Wolvercote Lock, is an Oxfordshire term for a channel carrying surplus water away from a main watercourse, but the word is also used to mean the weir by which the flow is controlled. North of the Lasher a stone wall is visible a few yards from the water's edge. This is the only reminder of the 13th century abbey of Rewley, and gives a reasonable approximation of the size of its grounds. The Lasher, called Ruley Lasher at times in the past, marked the southern extent, and a now lost stream the northern one. This water-course, at one time skirting the very walls of the Abbey, was still apparent in photos from the 1890s, and seems certain to have been the true Rewley Abbey Stream, a name sometimes wrongly attributed to the Sheepwash Channel. Like many of the Thames' rivulets and streams in Oxford ("more in number than your eyelashes", John Keats once wrote), it has now disap-peared beneath housing. Midway along the old Abbey wall, a fine **15th century watergate** is clearly visible from the canal.

The watercourse into which the culvert from Worcester College still feeds is called the Wareham Stream, and is thought to have been cut in the 15th century — just one of many attempts over time to divert and control the water on which the rival mills of the Castle and Osney Abbey depended. It is even possible that boats wishing to by-pass the Castle Mill used this as the main thoroughfare at times prior to the 18th century. The **Lasher** was referred to as Beesley's Lasher by Worcester College in 1913, the name deriving from Thomas Beesley, who first took over the tenancy of the property beside the Lasher in 1795. The Beesleys were just one of many families in Fisher Row (which extended in three sections all the way down to the Castle Mill) who could trace their connections with this locality back to the 17th cen-tury, when it was populated mostly by fishermen, whose sons and grandsons went on to prosper in the river-barge trade.

The Beesleys versus the Bossoms

The arrival of the Oxford Canal brought new opportunities — and new frictions — for this closely knit community of watermen. An early rift occurred between Thomas Beesley, who remained loyal to his river background, and his brother William, who switched his allegiance to the canal. A third main ingredient in the inter-family rivalries of the Row was the Bossom family, who had equally long associations with the area, and were the Beesleys' arch rivals in respect of trade on the river. An early indication of this occurs in *Jackson's Oxford Journal* for 26 January 1790, when a fight was noted "between two bargemen, Beasley and Bossom, over a difference on the river for a wager of 1 guinea". Coming just weeks after the canal reached the city, it is not inconceivable that their "difference" was occasioned through competing for the new trade that the canal offered. Ultimately the Bossoms moved out to establish a boatyard at Medley — albeit still dogged by the Beesleys, who had a rival concern on the opposite bank at least until the 1920s. The one remaining boatyard there is still known colloquially as Bossom's, even though there has been no connection with the family for quite some time.

The Beesleys remained to dominate the affairs of Fisher Row right up until World War Two. William had wide-ranging influence, derived from his unyielding control of the transhipment of goods between the canal and river. Like many other local men with backgrounds in the waterways, he also involved himself in brewing, being landlord of a pub called The Fishes on the site of today's **Antiquity Hall** pub at the turn of the 18th and 19th centuries. He also had a role in the construction of **Isis Lock**, since a payment to him of £10 5s 6d was noted in the Canal Company ledgers for 13 August 1796 "for carriage of stones" — who knows, possibly the same massive blocks which top either side of the lock even today.

It was the descendants of William's brother, Thomas, who gained particular fame, however, notably two of his grandsons, Abel and Jacob. From the middle of the 19th century, when trade on both the river and canal was hit by the arrival of the railways, the traditional boatmen of Oxford were obliged to find

Opposite:
Hythe Bridge Overflow, c. 1880, photographed by Henry Taunt. This wintry scene looking northwards from Hythe Bridge shows (middle left) the shed where Jacob Beesley ran his basket-making business, and some iced-in narrowboats on the canal (centre right). Beyond them are the trees of Worcester College.

Copyright: Oxfordshire County Council Photographic Archive

other occupations. The growth of water-based leisure pursuits offered one appropriate possibility, with punt racing proving especially popular. The Beesleys and Bossoms were foremost in this new sport, reviving their ancient rivalry by treating the races, in the words of Mary Prior, author of *Fisher Row*, as "something between the duel, the joust, and the prize-fight". Indeed the races had to be suspended in the 1860s owing to the excessive hostility of the competitors. When the sport was later regulated, Abel Beesley (living at No 4 Upper Fisher Row) emerged as its greatest professional exponent, becoming champion of England for six consecutive years in the 1880s before retiring undefeated.

Meanwhile Abel's cousin, Jacob Beesley, found another means by which to maintain the family's traditional connections with the river. The osier works he established on the land to the north of his house at No 12 Upper Fisher Row became highly successful, and a useful source of employment for local people. Here willow rods were woven into hampers, baskets, and traps for fish, eels, and crayfish. In *Ramlin Rose*, Sheila Stewart quotes one boatwoman as saying it was *"cruel work. Women and children used to pull the rads out of boilin' hot coppers and pull them through the stripping iron."*

The last Beesley to live in the Row was Jacob's daughter, May. When she married one Frank Jones in 1915, this famous boating name was lost to the locality. The land by the Lasher was sold for housing, the two semi-detached houses being the first Council houses in Oxford when built in 1919, according to Colin Tustin. Jones also sold off the long strip of land between the Abbey wall and Castle Mill Stream. To the Tustins, this is known as the Flam — Oxford dialect for a low, watery, rushy place. Jones was also the first person in the Row ever to own a car. Other residents were less progressive. Kath Tustin and Pat Weller both recalled the Hansom cab which was kept by a resident — reputedly the last of its kind in Oxford.

During the second world war, Ray Titcomb's father was one of the men who used to go out in a punt with Jones to scavenge for coal. It often spilled down to the water's edge near where the locomotives refuelled to the north of the Sheepwash Channel.

All those decades on from the arrival of that first coalboat, coal was still a commodity of paramount importance!

A housing shortage after the war resulted in dozens of families living afloat in Oxford. One such was the James family, who lived on a converted narrowboat moored at the Hythe Bridge end of Upper Fisher Row. There were several children, contemporaries of Ray Titcomb and his sister, Della James. One of the boys, Jack, went on to help establish the Waterways Museum at Stoke Bruern on the Grand Union Canal in Northamptonshire.

Pubs of Hythe Bridge Street

The building at the corner of Upper Fisher Row and Hythe Bridge Street — a spot known as "Thieving Corner" in the 18th century — was formerly a pub called The Running Horses. Like The Antiquity Hall opposite, it had traded under several different names over time, had its own stables for use by tow-horses and had largely been run by families with boating connections, certainly throughout the 19th and early 20th centuries. It had been known as The Racers, then The Race Horses in the 1820s and 1830s, when the landlady was William Beesley's granddaughter. It was later taken over by the Howkins, another family with a boating background. The pub closed in 1939, and, having been used as ARP lodgings during the war, was never re-opened.

The pub called **The Antiquity Hall** assumed this name in recent years but was previously known as The Nag's Head and prior to that, for most of the 19th century, as The Fishes. The influential William Beesley was its publican, possibly the first, in 1797, and it was run by his grand-nephew as late as 1863, having by then changed its name to one that had been in use since at least the early 1820s, The Nag's Head. As with today's Antiquity Hall, this name seems to have been adopted from a former nearby hostelry, because a pub called The Nag's Head had been built at 32 Lower Fisher Row in 1790, presumably to coincide with the arrival of the canal the same year. The pub seems always to have been a favourite with the boating community. In the *Flower of Gloster*, E. Temple Thurston's 1911 account of a narrowboat journey beginning at Oxford, The Nag's Head is referred to as the place to look "if yer ever want a bargee in

Oxford". Replacing two 17th century cottages, the present building was erected in 1939, with Aubrey Tustin (Pat Weller's father) as the landlord before and after. It was a sign of the declining importance of the boating clientele that no stables were retained when the new building went up, and that it was designed for the very first time to be entered from Hythe Bridge Street rather from Middle Fisher Row.

The original Antiquity Hall had stood mid-way along Hythe Bridge St, and was accessed by a gap in a stone wall, from which derived its alternative name of The Hole In The Wall. The Hall itself lay next to a Mansion House not dissimilar to the present pub, and probably acquired its name through the patronage of Thomas Hearne, an Oxford historian of the early 1700s, who was in the habit of joining other antiquaries there for a "pot and a pipe".

In the 1770s, the establishment seems to have been the property of St Thomas' parish, along with the workhouse it adjoined on the south side of Hythe Bridge Street. This institution, which extended for some 180 feet according to a survey of 1772, doubtless housed many an out-of-luck resident of Fisher Row in its time. Indeed, in a letter written to John Wesley in 1732, a concerned Methodist writes of the difficulties of two inmates with a name forever connected with the Row, mentioning his imminent intention to go "to hear the determination of a meeting of S. Thomas' Parish respecting separating Bossum and his wife".

Hythe Bridge Overflow

At the Hythe Bridge end of the canal Arm is an early 19th century brick weir. Known as the 'Armchair Weir' on account of its shape when viewed from Upper Fisher Row, it takes the canal overflow into Castle Mill Stream. A wooden floating chapel (illustrated opposite) was moored on the Stream here from 1839 till 1868. It was paid for by the coalmerchant Henry Ward, presumably the father of William who later donated the land for St Barnabas' Church in Jericho. Known as the Boatmen's Floating Chapel, it was built to seat a maximum of 150 people, with a service held every Sunday afternoon and Wednesday evening for boatmen and their families. During the week it was

Opposite:
The Boatman's Floating Chapel, c.1840–50. The chapel was moored on Castle Mill Steam opposite Upper Fisher Row from 1839 to 1868. Its condition in this picture suggests a date soon after it was built. Note the canal arch under Hythe Bridge Street (far left) and the old Hythe Bridge (which was rebuilt in 1861), St George's Tower within the Castle complex (centre top), and a side view of The Nag's Head in Middle Fisher Row (centre right). The chances are that a Beesley or a Bossom would be among the residents gathered on the Row!

Copyright: Oxfordshire County Council Photographic Archive

used as a school. The Chapel was sufficiently permanent to be named on Hoggar's 1850 map; but, despite contributions towards its upkeep from the Canal Company, it slowly decayed and in 1868 sank, having, according to the photographer Henry Taunt, "fulfilled its mission". In fact, it probably hadn't, quite, because it was replaced with a permanent chapel on the north side of Hythe Bridge Street. This building, now a Thai restaurant, was used for religious services until about 1892 and doubled as a day school for infants and a night school for the men.

The concave brickwork which strengthened the river bank where the chapel was moored is still apparent to the north of the overflow weir. Previously this had been the approximate location of a lock which briefly preceded Isis Lock as a link to the Thames in the 1790s. The first Canal Company Chain Survey, compiled immediately after the canal was completed in 1790, shows a "Lock onto Isis" at this point, and the same lock is clearly depicted in a painting of about 1790 by the London artist Michael Angelo Rucker. It is shown as a brick-built structure crossed by a wooden footbridge, set at an oblique angle to river and canal, and with a single pair of movable gates. It is clearly marked on a 1797 map by Richard Davis, "Cartographer to his Majesty", and subsequent paintings indicate its continued presence in an increasingly dilapidated state for another 40 years or so. It was in any case never satisfactory. In defending the rationale of building the double-gated pound lock which became Isis Lock, the Company minutes of 28 September 1792 refer to "injuries which have been repeatedly experienced from letting water out of the Basin". The simple flash lock depicted in Rooker's painting would have done exactly that — allowing boats to leave or enter the canal on a wave of suddenly freed water, much as the original Thames locks had.

Before stepping on to Hythe Bridge Street, it is worth pausing at the monument designed by William Bird in the somewhat inappropriate shape of a capstan wheel. It commemorates the canal's 200th anniversary — well, almost! The Oxford Canal was finished by December 1789, but this bicentennial monument was inaugurated in September 1993: as ever, the pace of life on the canal is slow! Ray Titcomb remembered the days when the canal was blocked off here in about 1950. With the Basin drained of its water, he and his schoolfriends carried floundering fish and eels from the mud on one side of Hythe Bridge to the canal on the other. The grassed area was the result of a job creation scheme in the late 1970s. One clue to the course the canal used to take remains: a single edging stone, nestling between tree roots.

 ## The City

Hythe Bridge and New Road Wharves (The Basin)

On the southern side of Hythe Bridge Street, a carpark presides where the Hythe Bridge Wharves once lay, while Nuffield College occupies the former New Road Basin. Before the arrival of the canal, these lands appear to have been largely undeveloped gardens, referred to in documents of the time as "W. Dunsford's House and Garden", "Badcock's Garden", or "Bossom's Garden". From the level of the cars, the position of the canal's entrance arch under Hythe Bridge Street can be discerned from the half a dozen or so bricks which formed the edge of the span, while on the far side, next to Rosie O'Grady's pub (formerly The Queen's Arms), stands the only other relic of the site's earlier use — a single blue brick pillar, which marks the former road access to the wharves.

The arrival of the first coalboat at these wharves instantly halved the cost of coal for the citizens of Oxford, and was an understandable cause of excitement. *Jackson's Oxford Journal* of 2 January 1790 reported the first coalboat unloading there amidst celebrations which included a band and an ox-roast. A few days later, on 7 January 1790, the ledgers of the parish church of St Thomas show a payment of 5s for bellringing as part of the "rejoicing at ye coals coming to Oxford to ye New Cannal Wharf".

In its early years, the Canal Company prospered. The cost of construction meant that no dividends were paid out in the first few years, but receipts leapt from £5,500 in 1789 to £26,000 in 1796, and, as we have seen, trade was such that the Company widened the arch of the bridge between the two wharves to

admit river barges in 1800. This little humpback bridge on Worcester Street survived until the construction of Nuffield College began around 1950. Nancy Sherratt and her four sisters lived in a house immediately next to this bridge from 1922 until the wharves were sold in 1937. Although their house, 'Wharf House', was situated within the Hythe Bridge site, her father, Bernard Robinson, was wharfinger at New Road, and she remembered how he would do the rounds of the dosshouses of St Thomas's parish whenever boats arrived, to enlist labour to unload them. Even in those depressed times, this hard, dirty, exposed work found few enthusiasts.

The Hythe Bridge site was run by Hubert Hawkins, and Nancy remembered her sisters' girlish infatuation with the handsome young man who used to load Hawkins' coalcart. It was pulled by an immensely patient, obedient horse called Blossom, who went all over Oxford to make deliveries. Hawkins, in fact, was married to a daughter of the noted punt champion of Upper Fisher Row, Abel Beesley. As for the boaters themselves, the girls had little contact — although Nancy's father did regularly invite one man in for tea. They knew him only as 'Old Blower', on account of a slight speech defect and strong regional accent which, in combination with a liberal use of swear words, often had the girls in fits of discreetly shared mirth.

After the first world war, with trade scarce, the Canal Company abandoned its hold on the city centre. The Company minutes of 18 September 1927 stated that "the Committee is of the opinion that having regard to the extent and value of the land contained in the New Road and Hythe Bridge Wharves .... it would be in the best interests of the Shareholders of the Company to dispose of the New Road and Hythe Bridge sites". It was another ten years before the sale was satisfactorily completed, with the purpose of building Oxford's newest college, and still longer again before the project was realised. Nuffield College was completed in 1960, and through the gateway on Worcester Street a symbolic reminder of former use can be seen in the form of the oblong pond within the college grounds.

Despite all the competition, the total tonnage carried on the Oxford Canal grew modestly until the first world war. One

Opposite:
New Road Wharf, 1930s. Canal House stands top right, slightly obscured by vegetation, with the wall of Bulwarks Lane dropping away from it beneath the new buildings of St Peter's College. Top left is the spire of the Wesley Memorial Church in New Inn Hall Street. At this time the wharf was run by Bernard Robinson, Nancy Sherratt's father. Close investigation shows that the two boats are *Friendship* and *Elizabeth*, owned by Jack Skinner's uncle and aunt, Joe and Rose Skinner.

reason was that a journey by boat was relatively smooth, making the canal a preferred choice for fragile cargoes (such as nitro-glycerine!). In addition, the canal basin offered superior storage facilities, notably a major pottery warehouse. Pickfords too had a furniture depository here, straddling one line of the 'L', as Nancy Sherratt called it, the point where the canal branched within the Hythe Bridge site to enable boats to turn. Pickfords in fact had been one of the largest canal carrying companies in the 19th century. It was a murder on one of their passenger services in 1839 which gave Colin Dexter the inspiration for his Inspector Morse novel, *The Wench is Dead*, set fictionally on the Oxford Canal.

Canal House

Behind Nuffield College is the unmistakable Greek portico frontage of the Canal Company's former headquarters, Canal House. It was designed and built in 1827 by Robert Tawney, who had been the Company's agent and engineer since 1794, and was a member of the family of entrepreneurs and philanthropists (and another with a background in the river trade) who were influential in the affairs of west Oxford for many generations. At the time Canal House was constructed, the Company was approaching the peak of its success, and the proprietors evidently felt sufficiently confident to attempt to rival the pomp of Oxford's colleges with an ostentatious building of their own — even if its orientation does make it seem curiously uncertain about facing the wharves it was built to oversee.

The closest view of Canal House is from Bulwarks Lane, an ancient, winding passage which follows the outer extent of the protective ditch which encircled the Castle Mound in mediaeval times. From here you can consider the originality of a building which looks for all the world like a two-storey brick warehouse from this side, yet resembles a three-storey, stone-built Greek temple from New Road! Atop the Doric columns of the portico is more evidence of a company brimming with confidence: a quirky cartouche of Britannia and a loaded boat next to the Radcliffe Camera. Britannia's shield bears the arms of the city, impaled with the arms of the University — alluding to the significant number of college dons among the Company's original subscribers. The name 'Coade' appears among the folds of Britannia's robes, and the cartouche is indeed an example of Coade Stone, a fabricated material which was invented in 1769 (and produced until around 1840, when the secret of its composition was apparently lost). Coade Stone was used for ornamental detail on many buildings at the time, being preferred to cut stone by many because of its supposed resistance to frost. Certainly, the sharpness of the carving on Canal House stands as testimony to its resilience to both the weather and 20th century acid pollution.

The Oxford Canal Company cartouche on Canal House: the figure of Britannia and the city arms impaled with the arms of the University, alongside the Church of St Mary-the-Virgin, the Radcliffe Camera, and a boat seemingly more at home on the river than the canal—an unlikely juxtaposition of church, trade, city, and academia, advertising a commercial joint venture.
Copyright: Mark Davies

The Company's original headquarters had been a plain-fronted building in New Inn Hall Street, built on the site of a house and garden owned by a Mrs Stuart (or Stewart). The ubiquitous Daniel Harris was involved, handling the transaction with Mrs Stuart (for £550) after having been authorised by the Company on 19 September 1795 to build "a House and Offices" there. This he did in 1797. Originally called Wyaston House, it was still owned by the Company in 1878. Renamed Linton House, it is now the entrance lodge to St Peter's College, while Canal House is the home of the College's Master.

Journey's end

It seems only right to leave the last word to the people to whom the canal really was everything. In terms of boathandling pedigree, the respective families of both Jack and Rose Skinner are among the most remarkable. They and their kind were the ones who laboured in all weathers, who lived and loved, and were born and died on the Cut; for whom it was a birthplace, a nursery, a classroom, a workplace, a morgue, and very occasionally a playground. Now in their seventies, and retired 'to the bank', Jack and Rose still go cruising every year, although they can't get used to the idea that they can moor up whenever they want, and take things slowly! *"We can't stop! We've got to keep moving! In the old days, even on Sundays, we always kept moving,"* says Rose. There were some leisure moments, though. "Sing-songs" in the pubs with other boaters are fondly remembered, and the cinema or the theatre in Oxford (where they sometimes went to see the same show several times over). Rose also remembered vividly her girlhood wonderment at seeing her first elephant, tethered in the stables of the Basin when a circus was in town.

Despite the near-constant hard work, the hazards, the dirt and the discomfort, they both say that given their time over again they would still choose to work the boats. With the waterways almost exclusively associated with leisure activities nowadays, it's nice to think that the likes of Jack and Rose can sit back now, smile, and remember *"We had fun sometimes too!"*

Jack and Rose Skinner, photographed on Mark Davies's boat near Isis Lock in June 1998.
Copyright: Mark Davies

Kingsley Belsten: various articles for the *Oxford Times*, 1964 to 1971

Karl Boardman: *Oxfordshire Sinners and Villains* (Alan Sutton, 1994)

Hugh Compton: *The Oxford Canal* (David and Charles, 1976)

C. and E. Hibbert (eds.): *The Encyclopaedia of Oxford* (Macmillan, 1988)

Herbert Hurst: *Oxford Topography* (Clarendon Press, 1899)

Mary Prior: *Fisher Row: Fishermen, Bargemen and Canal Boatmen 1500–1900* (Clarendon Press, 1982)

Catherine Robinson and Elspeth Buxton: *Hayfield Road: Nine Hundred Years of an Oxford Neighbourhood* (1993)

Thomas Squires (ed): *In West Oxford: Historical Notes and Pictures Concerning the Parish of St Thomas the Martyr* (Mowbray, 1928)

Sheila Stewart: *Ramlin Rose: The Boatwoman's Story* (Oxford University Press, 1993)

Fred S. Thacker: *The Thames Highway Volume II — Locks and Weirs* (1920, reprinted in 1968 by David and Charles)

The Victoria History of the County of Oxfordshire, Volume IV